PHONICS

Kindergarten

Printed in the U.S.A.

ISBN 978-0-544-26773-2

13 14 15 16 17 18 19 20   0928   22 21 20 19

4500756892   A B C D E F G

Core Skills Phonics

Grade K

Unit 1: Readiness Skills

Unit 2: Consonants

Unit 3: Short Vowels

© Houghton Mifflin Harcourt Publishing Company

Features

The *Core Skills Phonics* series provides skill-specific pages that link phonics with spelling and reading, allowing students to build language skills through integrated activities.

In *Core Skills Phonics*, you will find:

- Readiness Skills exercises that encourage children to pay attention to the printed page and to elements on the page that are important as they begin to read.

- Skill-specific exercises that introduce the sounds of the consonants and vowels.

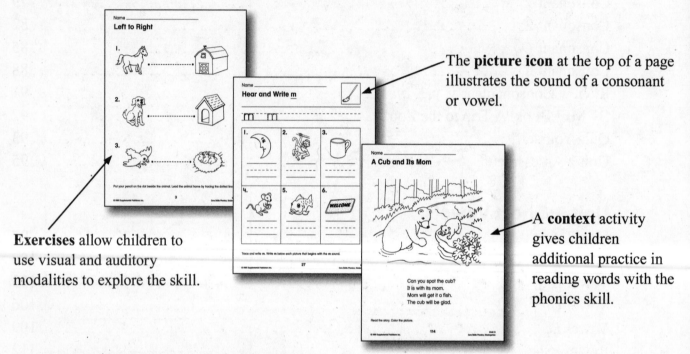

The **picture icon** at the top of a page illustrates the sound of a consonant or vowel.

A **context** activity gives children additional practice in reading words with the phonics skill.

Exercises allow children to use visual and auditory modalities to explore the skill.

Other features include the following:

- **reviews** to ensure that children have mastered the skill.

- a **By Me!** book at the end of each unit, which contains phonics-based words to develop reading comprehension. Children fold the page in half horizontally so that the print shows on both sides. Then they fold it in half again so that the cover faces up.

- **Quiz Yourself!**, an informal test of children's knowledge of the unit skills.

- a **unit assessment** to allow teachers to determine whether children have mastered the phonics skills.

- a **general assessment**, found on pages 1 and 2, which can be used as a diagnostic tool to gauge children's phonics knowledge before instruction or as a final test.

Name _____

General Assessment

1.	2.	3.

4.	5.	6.

7.	8.	9.

Write the letter that stands for the sound you hear at the beginning of each picture.

1

General Assessment, p. 2

1.	2.	3.
a i u	i e a	o e a

4.	5.	6.
e u a	u a e	o i e

7.	8.	9.
e a u	o u i	a e o

Circle the letter that stands for the vowel sound you hear in the picture.

General Assessment
Core Skills Phonics, Kindergarten

Left to Right

1.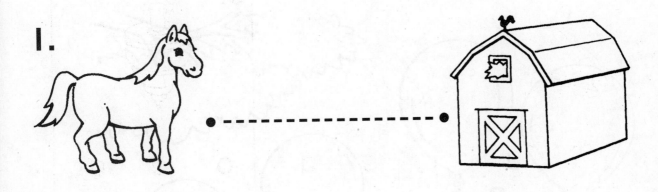

2.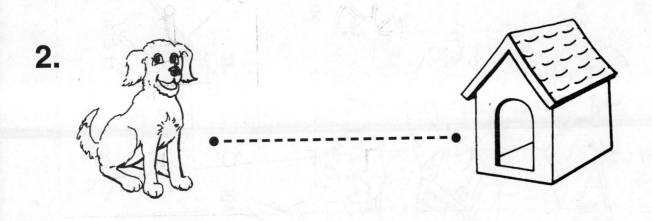

3.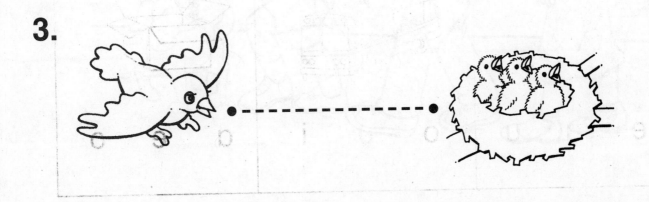

Put your pencil on the dot beside the animal. Lead the animal home by tracing the dotted line.

3

Top to Bottom

1. **2.** **3.** **4.**

Put your pencil on the dot below each balloon. Trace the line down to the one who is holding the balloon.

4

Circles

Put your pencil on each dot. Trace the dotted lines to complete the circles. Follow the arrows.
Color the picture.

Same

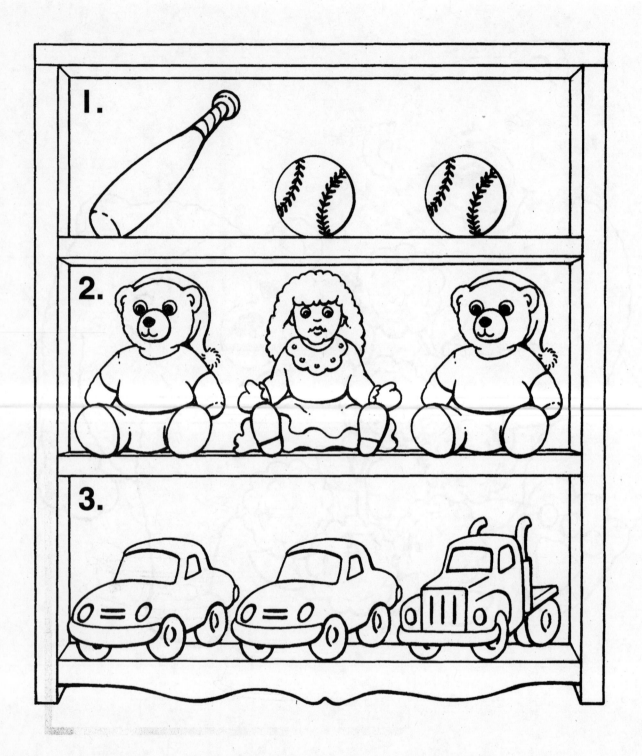

Color the two toys that are the **same** on each shelf.

Name _____

Different

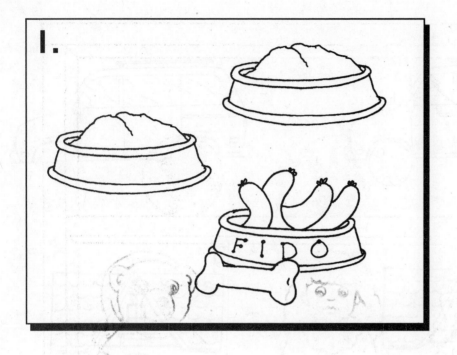

Color the bowl that looks **different** in each set.

Missing Parts

1.

2.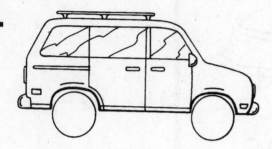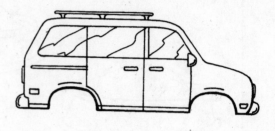

3.

Draw the missing parts to make each picture pair the **same**.

Reversals

1.

2.

3.

In each row, color the picture that is **different**.

9

Classification

I.

2.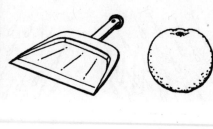

3.

Circle the picture that goes with each set.

Unit 1
Core Skills Phonics, Kindergarten

Name _____

Classification

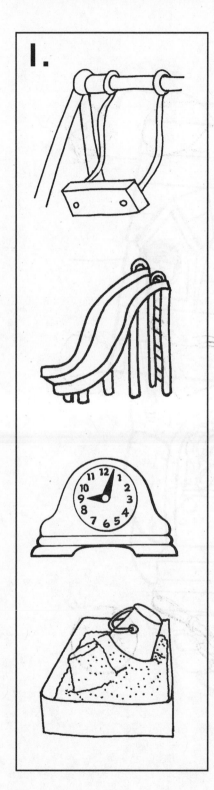

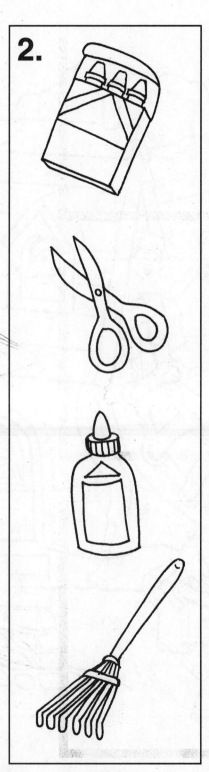

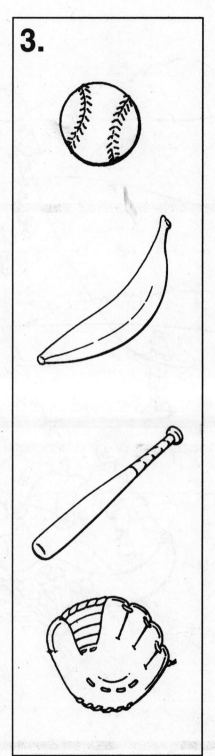

For each column, color the pictures that belong together.

Outside

Discuss the scene. Study the picture. Then color it. Circle the children who are playing **outside** the shoe.

12

Inside

Color each child who is **inside** a car.

Name _____

Above

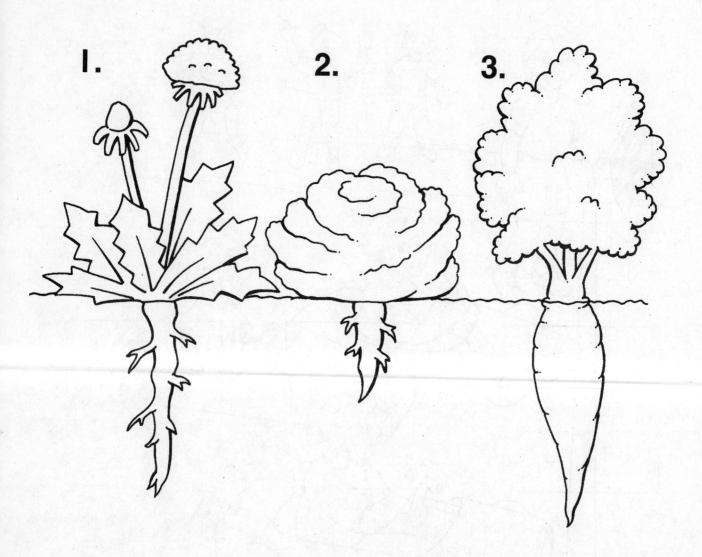

1. **2.** **3.**

Color the parts of the plants that are growing **above** the ground.

Unit 1

Core Skills Phonics, Kindergarten

Name _____

Below

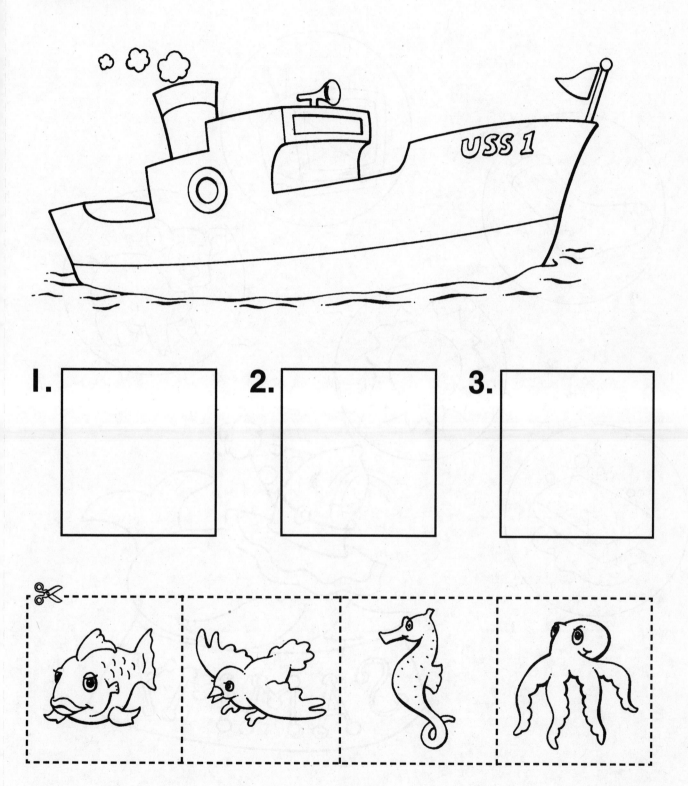

1.

2.

3.

Color the pictures and cut them out. Paste the animals that live **below** the ship in the squares.

Beginning Sounds

Color the seal. Color the pictures that **begin** with the same sound as the word **seal**.

16

Beginning Sounds

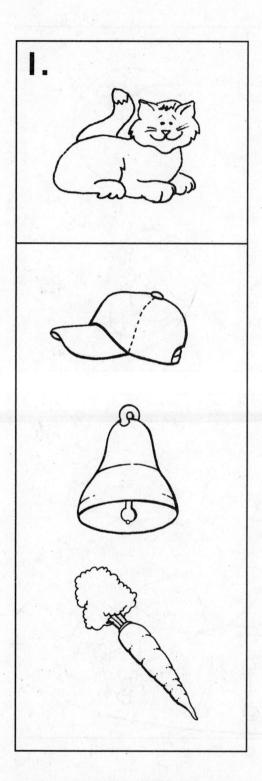

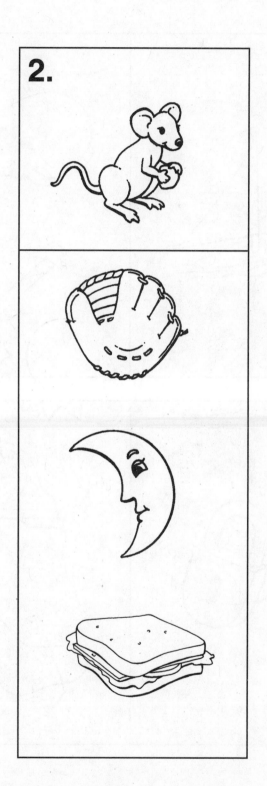

Color the pictures that **begin** with the same sound as the top picture in each column.

Rhyming Words

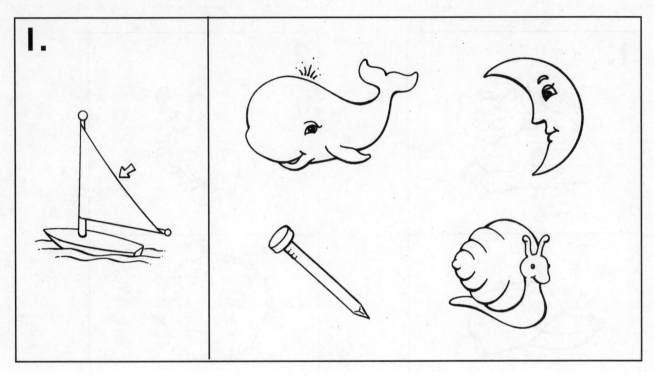

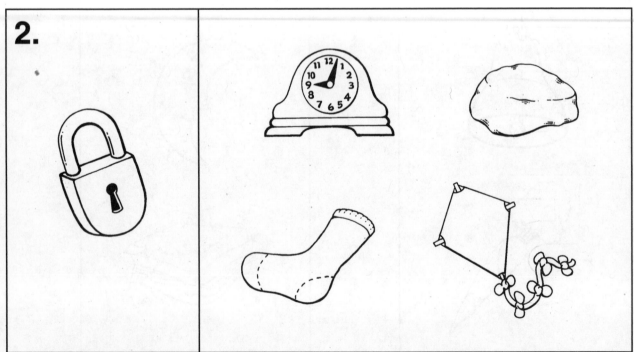

In each set, color the pictures that rhyme with the picture on the left.

18

Name _____

Rhyming Words

1. 2 •   •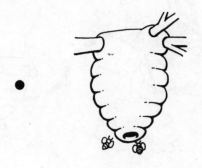

2. 3 •   •

3. 4 •   •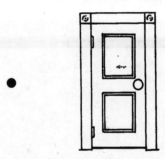

4. 5 •   •

Draw lines to match the pictures and numbers that rhyme. Color each number and picture that rhyme the same color.

19

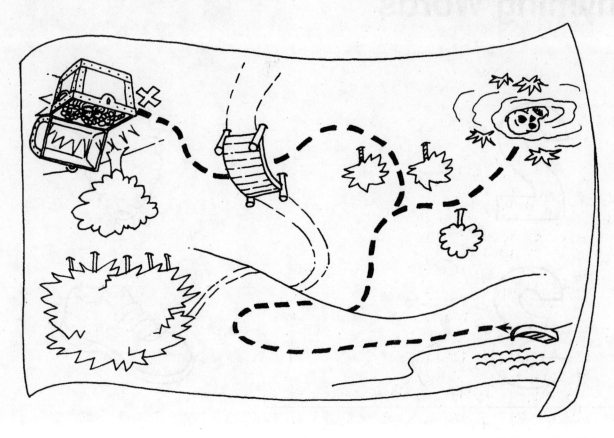

Can You Do It?

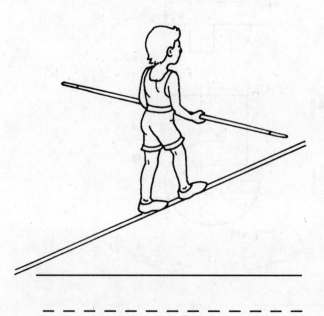

Follow the directions.

1. Connect the dots.
2. Draw a mouse outside the circle.
3. Draw some cheese inside the circle.
4. Draw a path from the mouse to the cheese.

made this book!

Name _____

Quiz Yourself!

I.

2.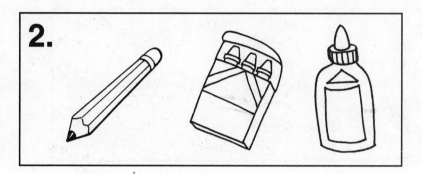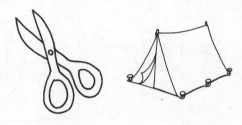

3.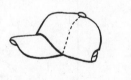

4.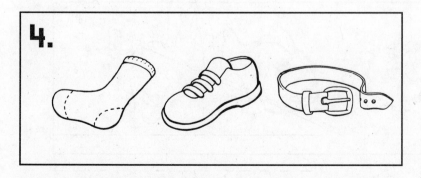

Circle the picture that goes with each set.

21

Quiz Yourself!, p. 2

1.

2.

3.

4.

Name the pictures in each row. Circle the picture that begins with the same sound as the first picture in each row.

22

Unit I Assessment

1.

2.

3.

4.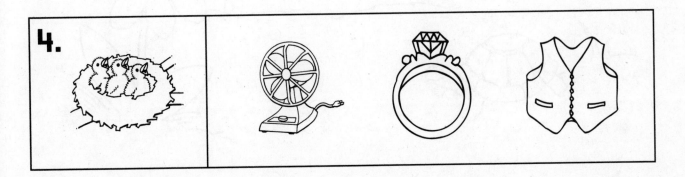

Name the pictures in each row. Circle the picture that rhymes with the first picture in each row.

Unit 1
Core Skills Phonics, Kindergarten

Unit I Assessment, p. 2

Place an X on the bird that is different. Use red to color the two flowers that are alike. Draw the missing part to complete the bee. Circle each living thing that can fly. Use any other colors to color the picture.

24

Name _____

See and Write <u>Mm</u>

M M - - - - - - - - - - - - - -

m m - - - - - - - - - - - - - -

Trace **M** and **m**. Write the letters on the lines. Use your yellow crayon to color the spaces with **M** or **m**. Use any other crayon to color the other spaces. Color the mice, too!

25

Unit 2

Core Skills Phonics, Kindergarten

Name _____

Listen for <u>M</u>m

M M M ― ― ― ― ― ― ― ― ― ― ― ― ― ―

m m m ― ― ― ― ― ― ― ― ― ― ― ― ― ―

1.

2.

3.

Trace and write **M** and **m**. Color the pictures that begin with the same sound as the word **mop**.

Name _____

Hear and Write m

m   m

1. 	2. 	3. 
4. 	5. 	6.

Trace and write **m**. Write **m** below each picture that begins with the **m** sound. Color the pictures.

Unit 2
Core Skills Phonics, Kindergarten

Name _____

See and Write Dd

D D -

d d -

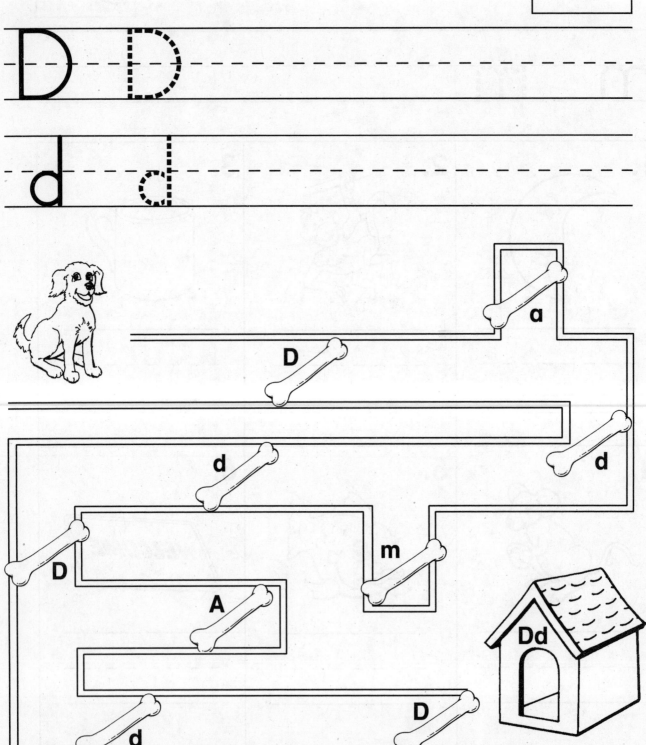

Trace **D** and **d**. Write the letters on the lines. Circle **D** and **d**. Start at the dog. Connect the circles you drew to get to the doghouse.

Name _____

Listen for D̲d̲

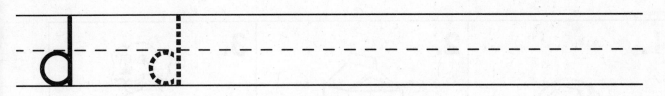

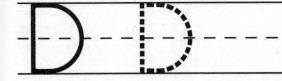

1.

2.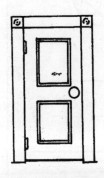

3.

Trace and write **D** and **d**. Color the pictures that begin with the same sound as the word **dog**.

29

Name _____

Hear and Write d

d   d

1.	2.	3.
	Milk Milk	
___	___	___
___	___	___

4.	5.	6.
___	___	___
___	___	___

Trace and write **d**. Write **d** below each picture that begins with the **d** sound. Color the pictures.

30

Unit 2
Core Skills Phonics, Kindergarten

Name _____

See and Write <u>Ff</u>

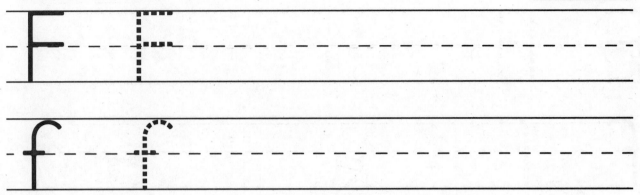

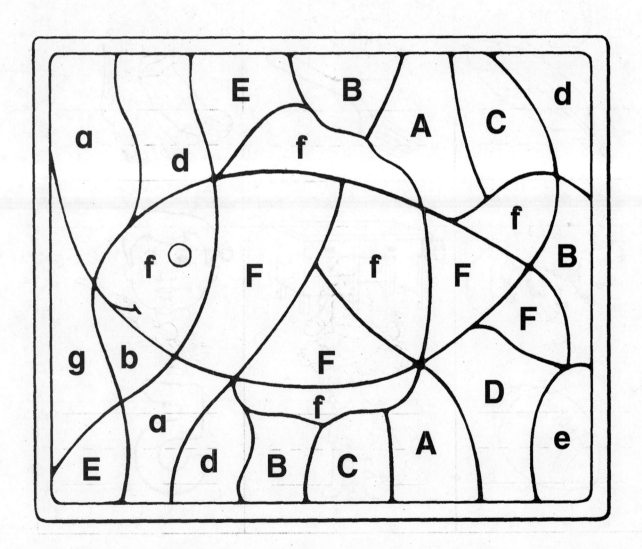

Trace **F** and **f**. Write the letters on the lines. Use your orange crayon to color the spaces with **F** or **f**. Use your blue crayon to color the other spaces.

31

Name _____

Listen for Ff

F F - - - - - - - - - - - - - - - -

f f - - - - - - - - - - - - - - - -

1.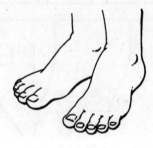

2.

3.

Trace and write **F** and **f**. Color the pictures that begin with the same sound as the word **fan**.

Name _____

Hear and Write f

f f —— —— —— —— —— —— —— ——

1.	2.	3.
———————	———————	———————
- - - - - - -	- - - - - - -	- - - - - - -
———————	———————	———————

4.	5.	6.
———————	———————	———————
- - - - - - -	- - - - - - -	- - - - - - -
———————	———————	———————

Trace and write **f**. Write **f** below each picture that begins with the **f** sound. Color the pictures.

33

See and Write <u>Gg</u>

G G ⟨G⟩

g g ⟨g⟩

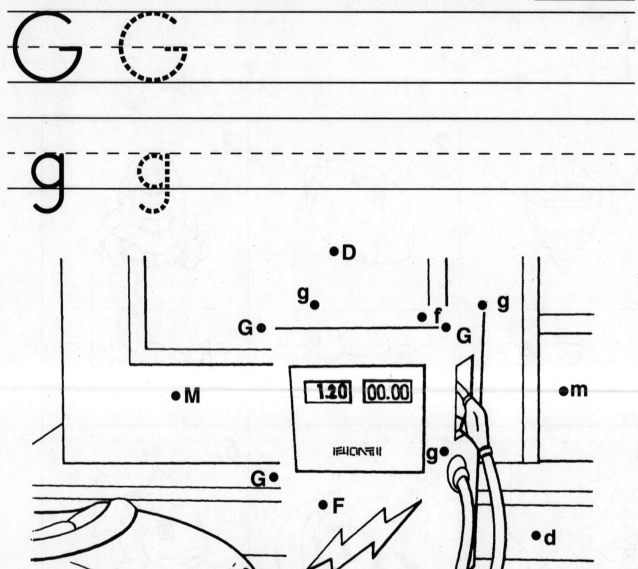

Trace **G** and **g**. Write the letters on the lines. Circle **G** and **g**. Put your pencil on the star. Connect the circles you drew to complete the picture. Color the picture.

34

Name _____

Listen for <u>Gg</u>

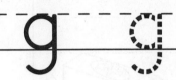

1.

2.

3.

Trace and write **G** and **g**. Color the pictures that begin with the same sound as the word **gas**.

35

Name ______________________

Hear and Write g

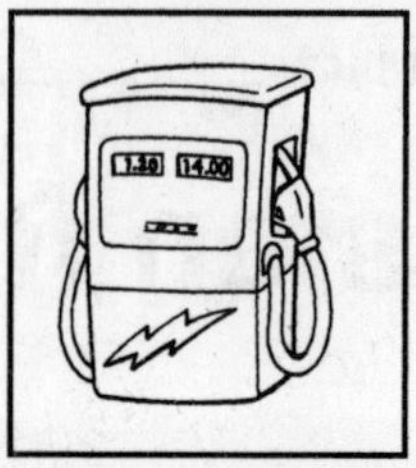

g g

1. 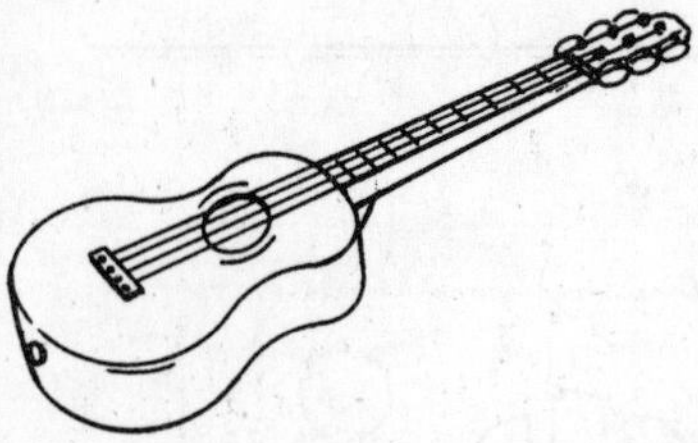	2. 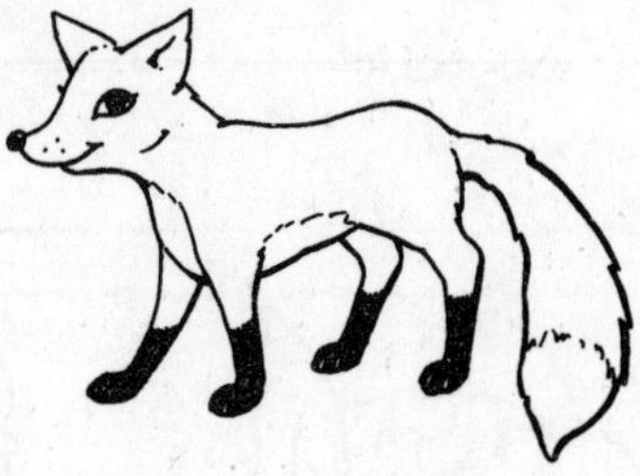	3. 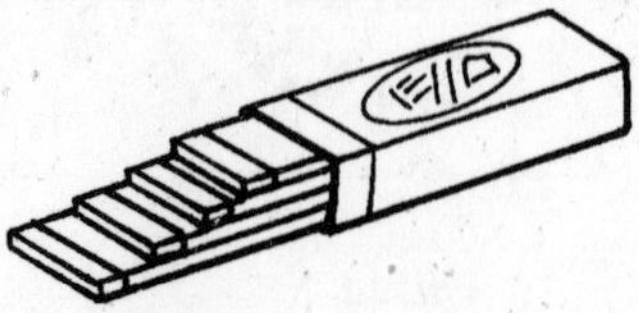
4. 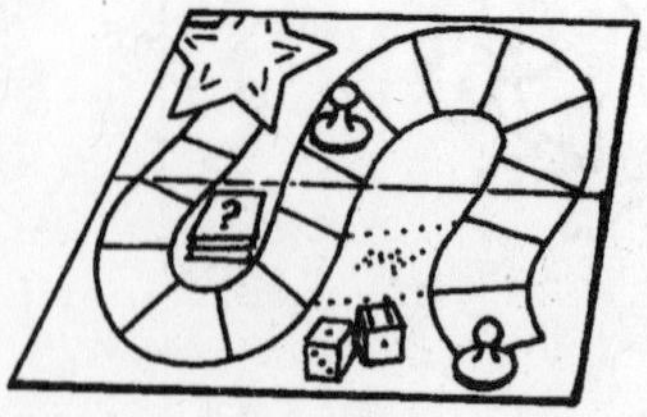	5. 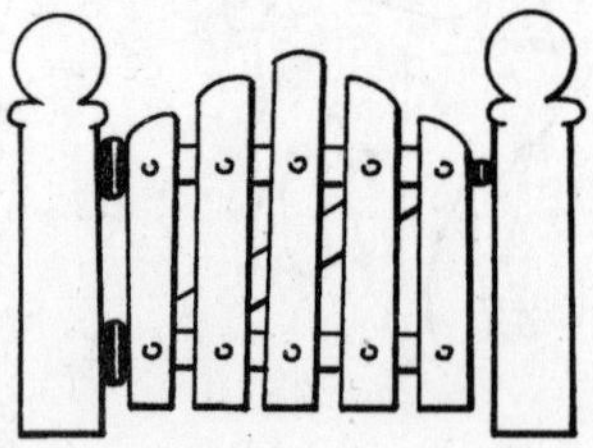	6. 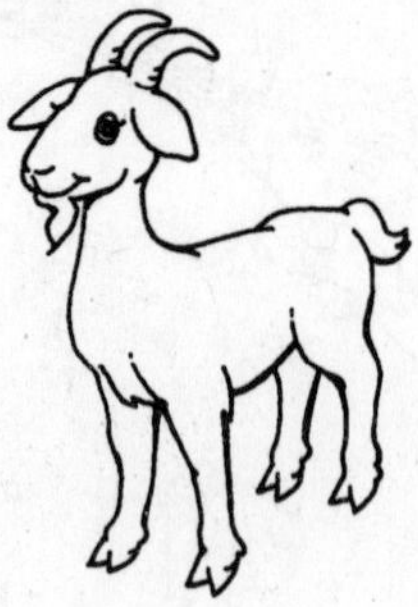

Trace and write **g**. Write **g** below each picture that begins with the **g** sound. Color the pictures.

Name _____

See and Write <u>Bb</u>

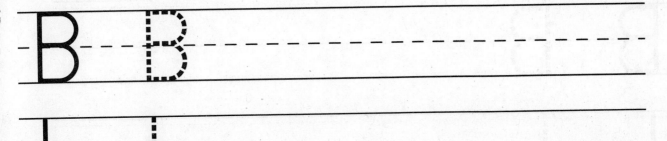

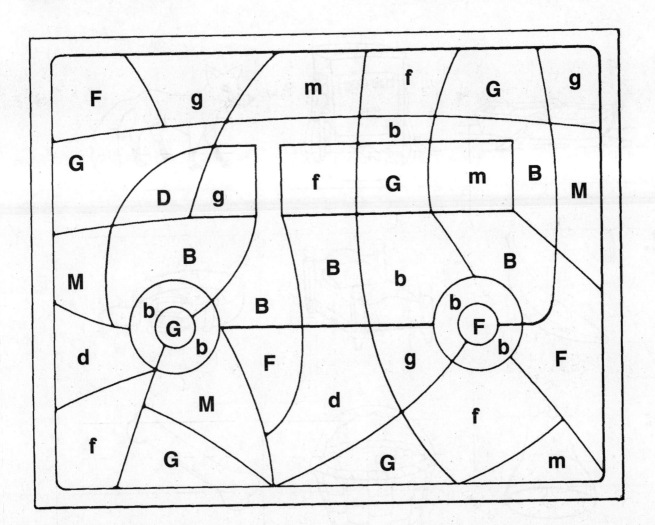

Trace **B** and **b**. Write the letters on the lines. Use your yellow crayon to color the spaces with
B or **b**. Use any other crayon to color the other spaces.

Name _____

Listen for Bb

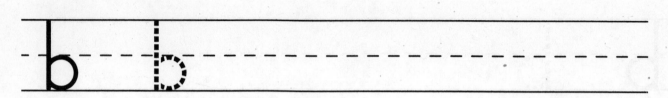

1.

2.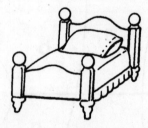

3.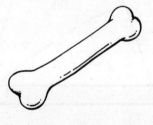

Trace and write **B** and **b**. Color the pictures that begin with the same sound as the word **bike**.

Unit 2
Core Skills Phonics, Kindergarten

Name _____

Hear and Write b

b b - - - - - - - - - - - - - - - - - - -

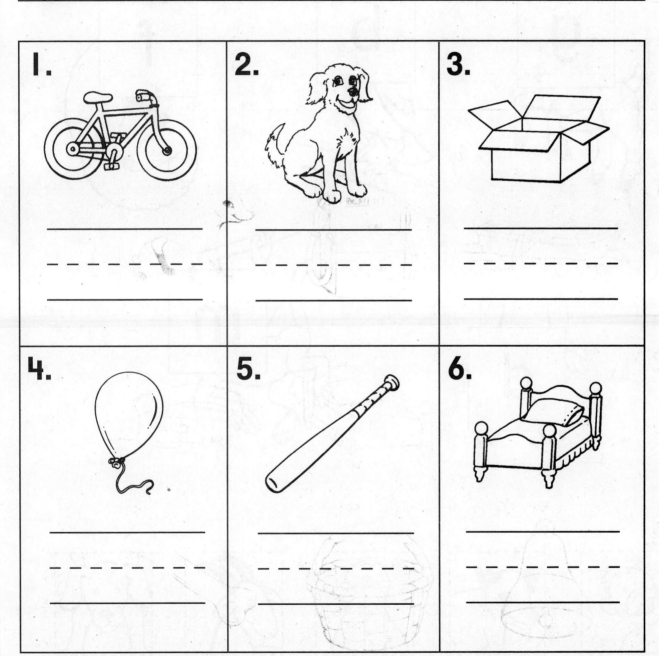

Trace and write **b**. Write **b** below each picture that begins with the **b** sound. Color the pictures.

Unit 2
Core Skills Phonics, Kindergarten

Name _____

Review Consonants <u>m</u>, <u>d</u>, <u>f</u>, <u>g</u>, <u>b</u>

Color the pictures and cut them out. Paste the heads on the bodies. Paste the puppets on sticks. Then make up a play about the animals.

Unit 2

Core Skills Phonics, Kindergarten

See and Write T̲t̲

d	F	m
M	t	T	t	D
	f		d	f
D			M	
f	M	t	F	
				D
m		T	m	
	d			
f	T	M	

Trace **T** and **t**. Write the letters on the lines. Use your blue crayon to color the spaces with **T** or **t**. Use any other crayon to color the other spaces. Color the turtles.

41

Name _____

Listen for Tt

T T

t t

1.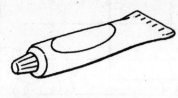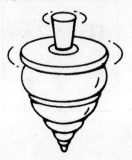

2.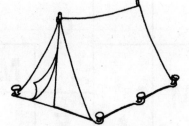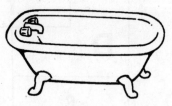

3.

Trace and write **T** and **t**. Color the pictures that begin with the same sound as the word **turtle**.

Unit 2
Core Skills Phonics, Kindergarten

Name _____

Hear and Write t

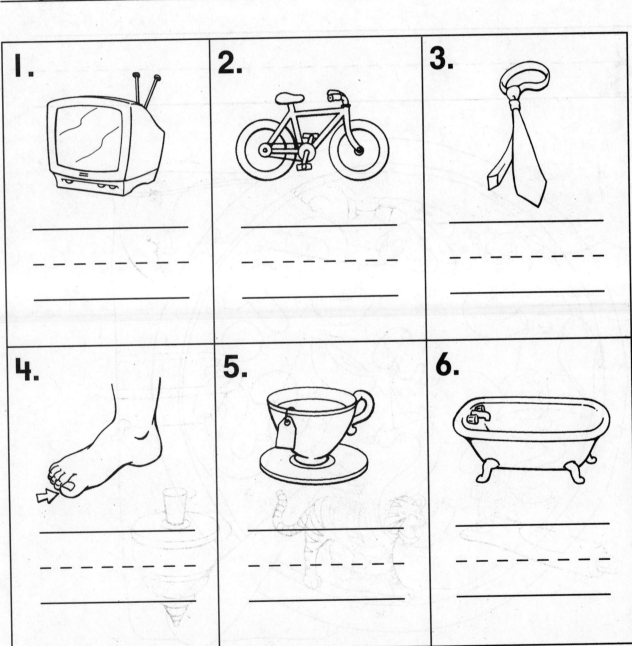

1.

2.

3.

4.

5.

6.

Trace and write t. Write t below each picture that begins with the t sound. Color the pictures.

Unit 2
Core Skills Phonics, Kindergarten

Name _____

See and Write S̲s̲

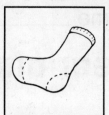

S   S

s   s

Trace **S** and **s**. Write the letters on the lines. Use your orange crayon to color **S** and **s** in the soup. Use any other crayons to color the rest of the picture.

44

Name _____

Listen for <u>S</u>s

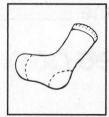

S S

s s

1.

2.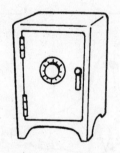

3.

Trace and write **S** and **s**. Color the pictures that begin with the same sound as the word **sock**.

Unit 2
Core Skills Phonics, Kindergarten

Name _____

Hear and Write s

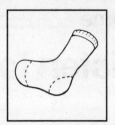

S   S

| 1.  | 2.  | 3.  |
| 4. 7 | 5.  | 6.  |

Trace and write **s**. Write **s** below each picture that begins with the **s** sound. Color the pictures.

© Houghton Mifflin Harcourt Publishing Company

Unit 2
Core Skills Phonics, Kindergarten

Name _____

See and Write <u>Ww</u>

W w

w w

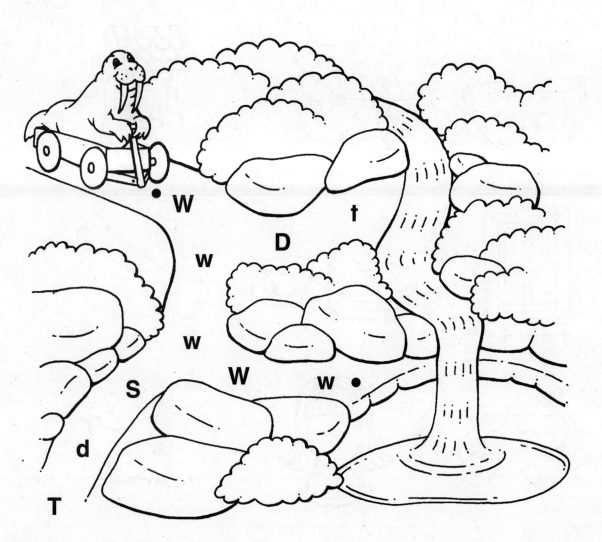

Trace **W** and **w**. Write the letters on the lines. Circle **W** and **w**. Start with the walrus. Connect the circles you drew to get to the waterfall. Color the picture.

Unit 2

Core Skills Phonics, Kindergarten

Name _____

Listen for Ww

W w —————————————————

w w ———————————————————

I.

2.

3.

Trace and write **W** and **w**. Color the pictures that begin with the same sound as the word **watch**.

48

Hear and Write w

W   w

1. 	2. 	3. 
4. 	5.	6. 

Trace and write **w**. Write **w** below each picture that begins with the **w** sound. Color the pictures.

Name _____

See and Write <u>Kk</u>

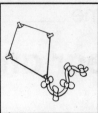

K — — K — — — — — — — — — — — — —

k — — k — — — — — — — — — — — — —

f G   B   F   b
   D   K   M   g
M   M   k
      k   f   D
   b   K   F
d   K   b
   m   m
G   m   k   d
   k
   F B   f   g   b   F
g

Trace **K** and **k**. Write the letters on the lines. Use your blue crayon to color the spaces with **K** or **k**. Use any other crayon to color the other spaces. Color the kites.

50

Core Skills Phonics, Kindergarten

Name _____

Listen for <u>K</u>k

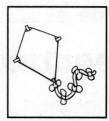

K K

k k

I.

2.

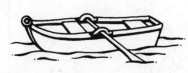  

3.

Trace and write **K** and **k**. Color the pictures that begin with the same sound as the word **kite**.

51

Hear and Write k

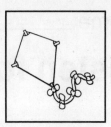

k   k

1.	**2.**	**3.**
4.	**5.**	**6.**

Trace and write **k**. Write **k** below each picture that begins with the **k** sound. Color the pictures.

Name _____

See and Write <u>J</u>j

J J J

j j j

Trace **J** and **j**. Write the letters on the lines. Circle **J** and **j**. Start at the jeep. Connect the circles you drew to get to the jungle.

53

Unit 2
Core Skills Phonics, Kindergarten

Listen for <u>J</u>j

J J

j j

1.

2.  **7**

3.

Trace and write **J** and **j**. Color the pictures that begin with the same sound as the word **jeep**.

Name _____

Hear and Write <u>j</u>

j j _____

1. 	2. 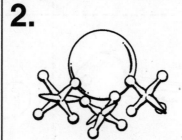	3. 
_____	_____	_____
- - - - - -	- - - - - -	- - - - - -
_____	_____	_____
4. 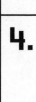	5. 	6. 
_____	_____	_____
- - - - - -	- - - - - -	- - - - - -
_____	_____	_____

Trace and write **j**. Write **j** below each picture that begins with the **j** sound. Color the pictures.

55

Review Consonants t̲, s̲, w̲, k̲, j̲

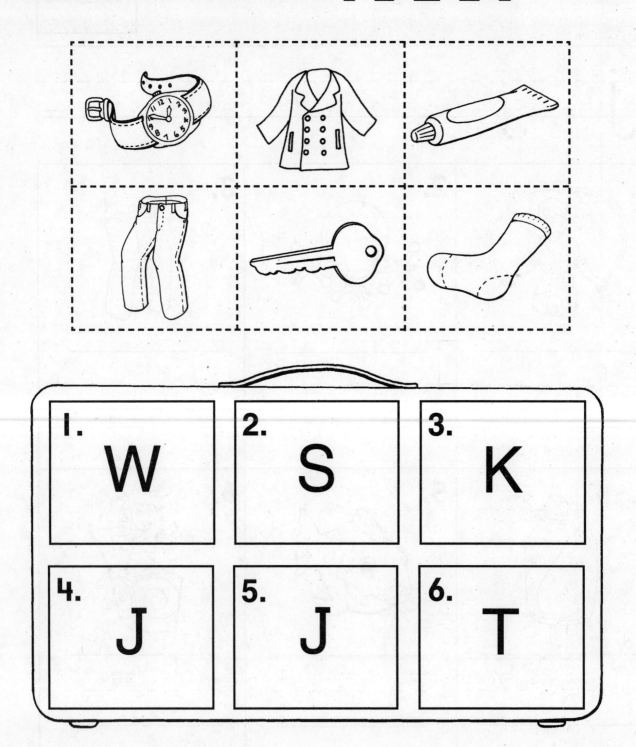

1. W
2. S
3. K
4. J
5. J
6. T

Color the pictures and cut them out. Match the beginning sound of each picture with a letter in the suitcase. Paste the picture on the letter. After your suitcase is packed, think about where you want to go.

56

Name _____

See and Write <u>P</u>p

P   P -

p   p -

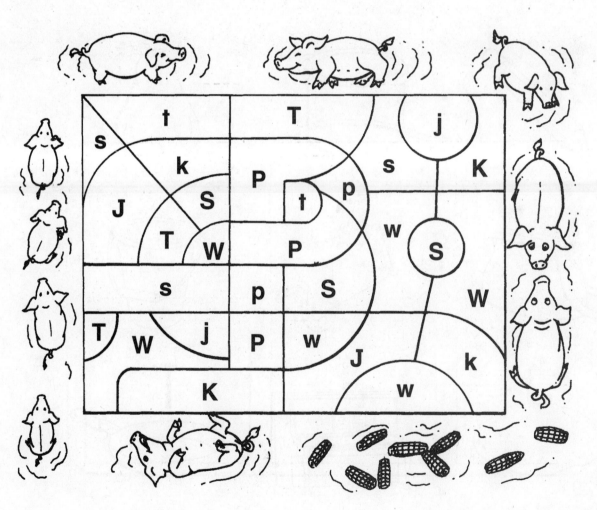

Trace **P** and **p**. Write the letters on the lines. Use your purple crayon to color the spaces with **P** or **p**. Use your green crayon to color the other spaces. Color the pigs.

57

Name _____

Listen for P<u>p</u>

P P - - - - - - - - - - - - - -

p p - - - - - - - - - - - - - -

I.

2.

 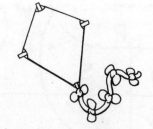 

3.

 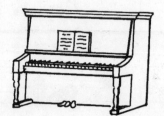 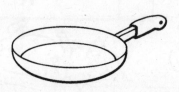

Trace and write **P** and **p**. Color the pictures that begin with the same sound as the word **pig**.

58

Hear and Write p

p p

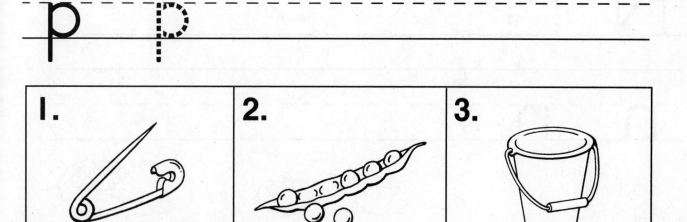

1.	2.	3.

4.	5.	6.

Trace and write **p**. Write **p** below each picture that begins with the **p** sound. Color the pictures.

59

Unit 2
Core Skills Phonics, Kindergarten

See and Write Nn

N N

n n

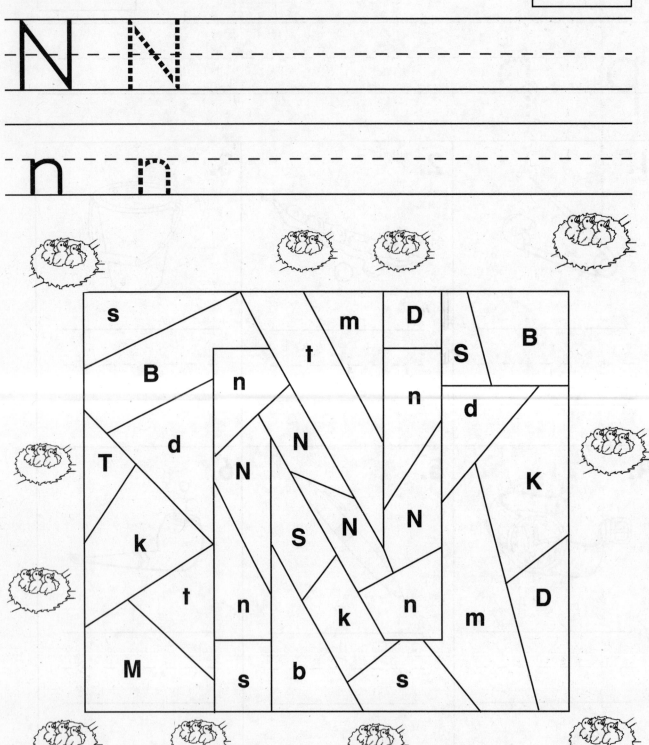

Trace **N** and **n**. Write the letters on the lines. Use your yellow crayon to color the spaces with **N** or **n**. Use any other crayon to color the other spaces.

60

Name _____

Listen for Nn

N N _ _ _ _ _ _ _ _ _ _ _ _ _ _ _ _

n n _ _ _ _ _ _ _ _ _ _ _ _ _ _ _ _

1.

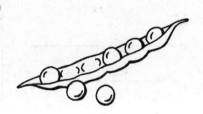  

2.

3.

Trace and write **N** and **n**. Color the pictures that begin with the same sound as the word **nest**.

61

Name _____

Hear and Write n

n n

1.	2.	3.
_____	_____	_____
- - - -	- - - -	- - - -
_____	_____	_____

4.	5.	6.
DAILY VIEW		
_____	_____	_____
- - - -	- - - -	- - - -
_____	_____	_____

Trace and write **n**. Write **n** below each picture that begins with the **n** sound. Color the pictures.

Core Skills Phonics, Kindergarten

Name _____

Listen for <u>H</u>h

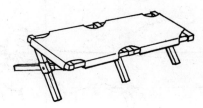

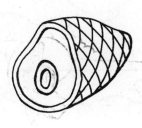

1.

2.

3.

Trace and write **H** and **h**. Color the pictures that begin with the same sound as the word **hat**.

67

Hear and Write h

h h

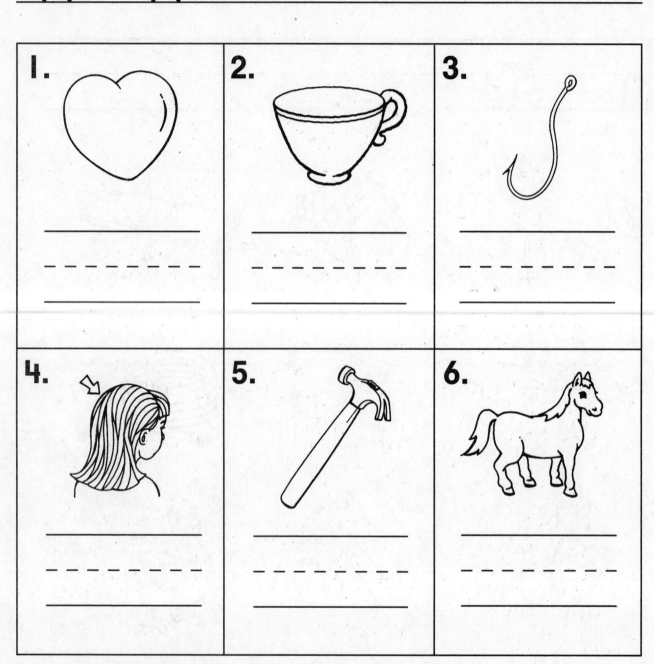

| 1. | 2. | 3. |
| 4. | 5. | 6. |

Trace and write **h**. Write **h** below each picture that begins with the **h** sound. Color the pictures.

Unit 2
Core Skills Phonics, Kindergarten

Name _____

See and Write L l

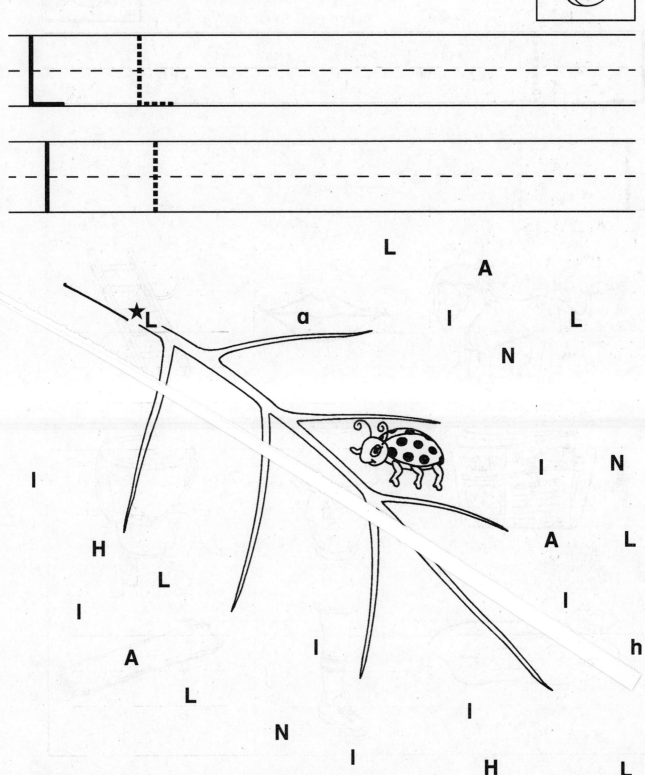

Trace **L** and **l**. Write the letters on the lines. Circle **L** and **l**. Put your pencil on the star. Connect the circles you drew to complete the picture. Color the picture.

69

Name _____

Listen for Ll

1.

2.

3.

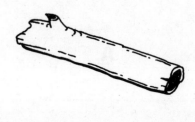

Trace and write **L** and **l**. Color the pictures that begin with the same sound as the word **lock**.

Unit 2

Core Skills Phonics, Kindergarten

Name _____

Hear and Write l

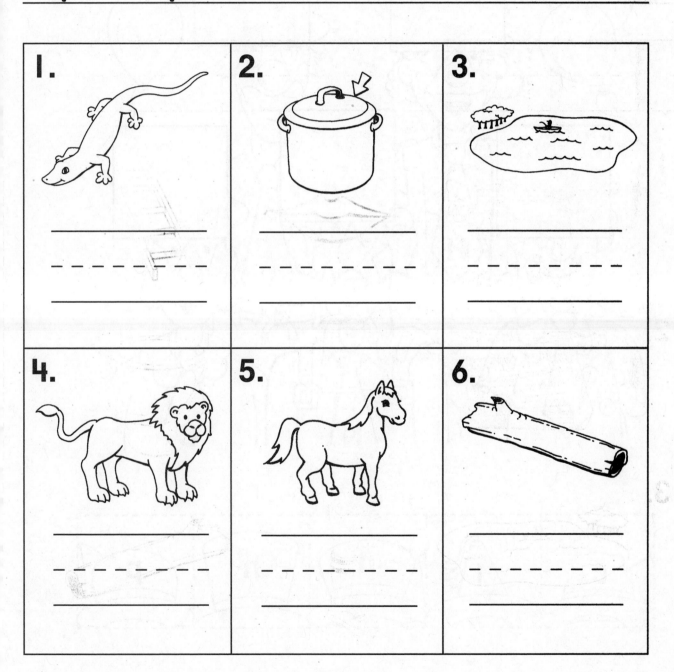

1.	2.	3.

4.	5.	6.

Trace and write l. Write l below each picture that begins with the l sound. Color the pictures.

71

Review Consonants p, n, c, h, l

Color the pictures and cut them out. Match the letter on each hat with the letter on a clown's tie. Paste the hats on the clowns. Then tell a funny joke.

72

Name _____

See and Write Rr

R R — — — — — — — — — — — — —

r r — — — — — — — — — — — — —

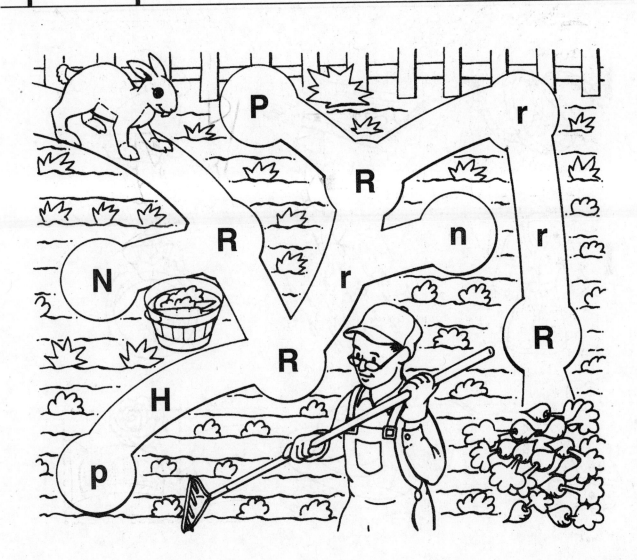

Trace **R** and **r**. Write the letters on the lines. Circle **R** and **r**. Start at the rabbit. Connect the circles you drew to get to the radishes. Color the picture.

73

Unit 2
Core Skills Phonics, Kindergarten

Name _____

Listen for R<u>r</u>

R----R--------------------

r----r--------------------

1.

 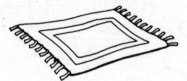 

2.

3.

Trace and write **R** and **r**. Color the pictures that begin with the same sound as the word **rake**.

Unit 2

Core Skills Phonics, Kindergarten

Name _____

Hear and Write r

r   r   r

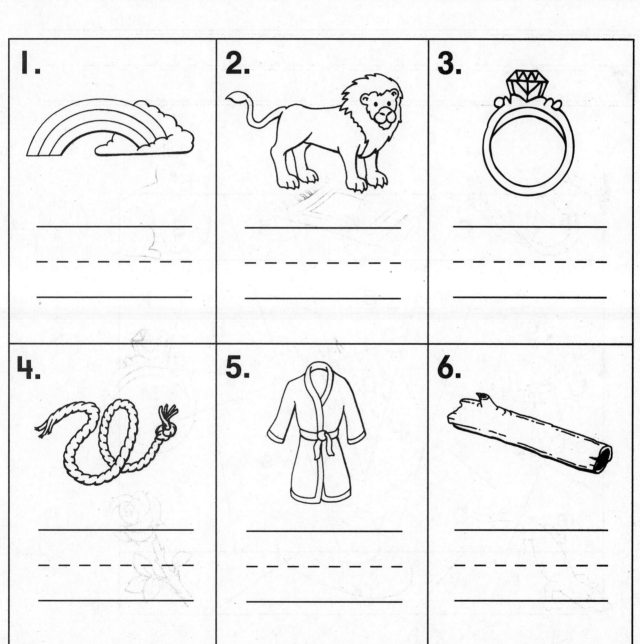

1.

2.

3.

4.

5.

6.

Trace and write **r**. Write **r** below each picture that begins with the **r** sound. Color the pictures.

Name _____

See and Write Vv

V V V

v v v

m	F	K	d	S
	g	V	B	v		k
	S			H
F		D	v	M
s	p	T	v	s
m	D	V	f
f	k	h

Trace **V** and **v**. Write the letters on the lines. Use your blue crayon to color the spaces with **V** or **v**. Use your red crayon to color the other spaces. Color the vests.

Unit 2
Core Skills Phonics, Kindergarten

Name _____

Listen for <u>Vv</u>

V V ⌐⌐ V

v v ⌐⌐ v

1.

2.

3.

Trace and write **V** and **v**. Color the pictures that begin with the same sound as the word **vest**.

77

Name _____

Hear and Write v

V V V

1. Be mine	**2.**	**3.**
_____ - - - - - - - _____	_____ - - - - - - - _____	_____ - - - - - - - _____
4.	**5.**	**6.**
_____ _____ _____	_____ _____ _____	_____ _____ _____

Trace and write **v**. Write **v** below each picture that begins with the **v** sound. Color the pictures.

78

Core Skills Phonics, Kindergarten

Name _____

See and Write <u>Yy</u>

Y   Y

y   y

Trace **Y** and **y**. Write the letters on the lines. Use your yellow crayon to color the pictures with **Y** or **y**. Use any other crayon to color the other pictures.

Unit 2
Core Skills Phonics, Kindergarten

Name _____

Listen for <u>Y</u>y

Y   Y

y   y

I.

  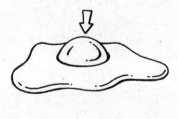

2.

 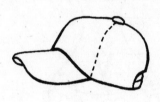 

3.

Trace and write **Y** and **y**. Color the pictures that begin with the same sound as the word **yarn**.

80

Name _____

Hear and Write y

y y y

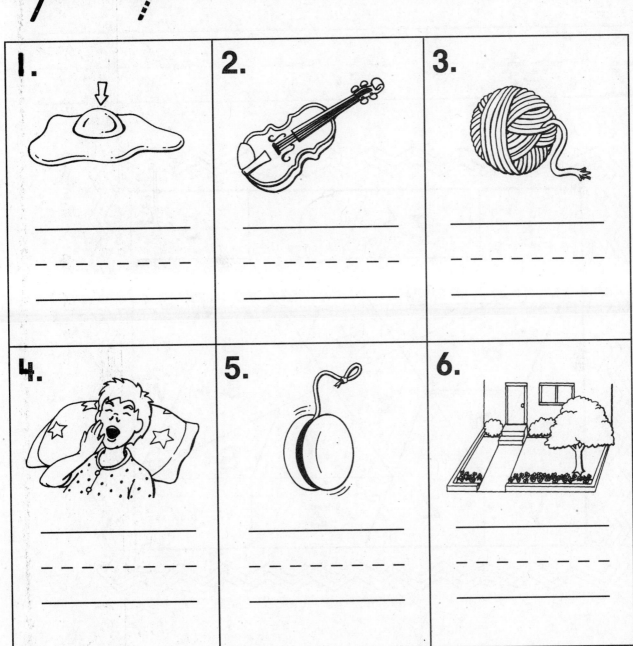

1.

2.

3.

4.

5.

6.

Trace and write **y**. Write **y** below each picture that begins with the **y** sound. Color the pictures.

© Houghton Mifflin Harcourt Publishing Company

Unit 2
Core Skills Phonics, Kindergarten

Name _____

See and Write Z̲z

Z z — — — — — — — — — — — —

z z - - - - - - - - - - - - - - -

Trace **Z** and **z**. Write the letters on the lines. Use your red crayon to color the spaces with **Z** or **z**.
Use any other crayon to color the other spaces.

82

Name _____

Listen for Zz

Z   Z

Z   z

I.

2.

3.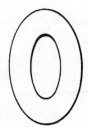

Trace and write **Z** and **z**. Color the pictures that begin with the same sound as the word **zipper**.

83

Name _____

Hear and Write z

z   z

1.

_____

- - - - - - - - - - -

_____

2.

_____

- - - - - - - - - - -

_____

3.

_____

- - - - - - - - - - -

_____

4.

_____

- - - - - - - - - - -

_____

5.

_____

- - - - - - - - - - -

_____

6.

_____

- - - - - - - - - - -

_____

Trace and write **z**. Write **z** below each picture that begins with the **z** sound. Color the pictures.

Unit 2
Core Skills Phonics, Kindergarten

Name _____

See and Write <u>Qq</u>

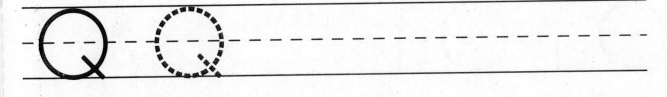

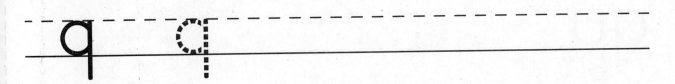

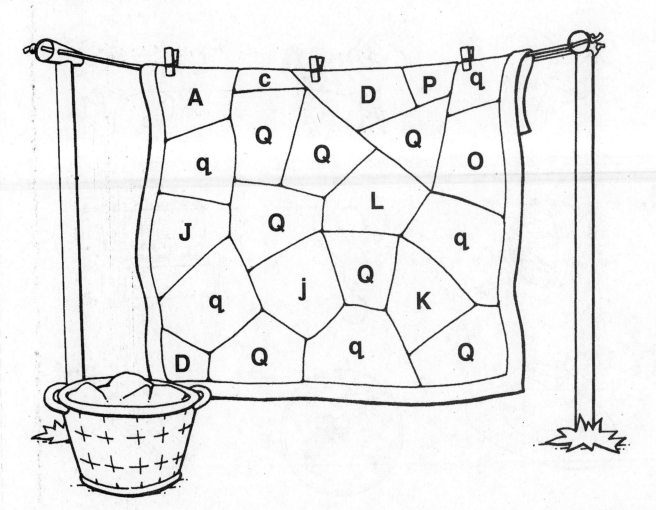

Trace **Q** and **q**. Write the letters on the lines. Use your yellow crayon to color the spaces with **Q** or **q**. Use any other crayon to color the other spaces.

Unit 2
Core Skills Phonics, Kindergarten

Name _____

Listen for <u>Qu</u>

Qu Qu _____

qu qu _____

1.

2.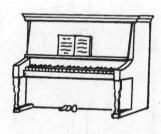

3.

The letters **q** and **u** always go together. Listen for the sound of **qu** in **quilt**. Trace and write **Qu** and **qu**. Color the pictures that begin with the same sound as the word **quilt**.

86

Name _____

Hear and Write <u>qu</u>

qu qu _____

1. 	**2.** 	**3.** 
___ ___ ___	___ ___ ___	___ ___ ___
4. 	**5.** 	**6.** 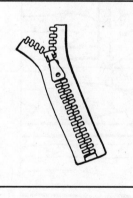
___ ___ ___	___ ___ ___	___ ___ ___

Trace and write **qu**. Write **qu** below each picture that begins with the **qu** sound. Color the pictures.

87

Name _____

See and Write <u>Xx</u>

X   X

X   X

Trace **X** and **x**. Write the letters on the lines. Use your brown crayon to color the spaces with **X** or **x**. Use your green crayon to color the other spaces.

88

Listen for <u>X</u>x

X X

X x

1.

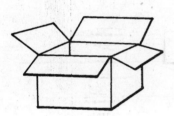

2.

3.

Trace and write **X** and **x**. Color the pictures that end with the same sound as the word **ax**.

Name _____

Hear and Write <u>x</u>

X   X

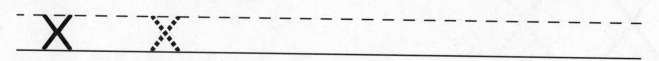

1.

_____
- - - - - - - - -
_____

2.

_____
- - - - - - - - -
_____

3.

_____
- - - - - - - - -
_____

4.

_____
- - - - - - - - -
_____

5.

_____
- - - - - - - - -
_____

6.

_____
- - - - - - - - -
_____

Trace and write **x**. Write **x** below each picture that ends with the sound of **x**. Color the pictures.

90

Unit 2
Core Skills Phonics, Kindergarten

Name _____

Review Consonants r, v, y, z, qu

Color the pictures and cut them out. Paste each picture over the beginning consonant you hear in its name. Make up a sentence about the artist.

© Houghton Mifflin Harcourt Publishing Company

A Trip to the Zoo!

_____

- - - - - - - - - - - -

_____

made this book!

Oh, No! Now we can't go!

Name _____

Quiz Yourself!

1. **M**	k p m	2. **Z**	z s n
3. **V**	w v y	4. **P**	r w p
5. **H**	j h b	6. **F**	r l f
7. **D**	g c d	8. **Q**	q b k

In each box, circle the letter that is the partner of the first letter.

93

Quiz Yourself!, p. 2

1. s	

2. b	

3. l	

4. r	

Name the letter and pictures in each row. Circle the picture whose name begins with the sound that the letter stands for.

Unit 2

Core Skills Phonics, Kindergarten

Name _____

Unit 2 Assessment

1. **G**	b g d	**2.** **R**	n r s
3. m	M W P	**4.** **F**	f h t
5. **X**	v w x	**6.** b	H B G
7. **D**	d g h	**8.** **T**	l t j

In each box, circle the letter that is the partner of the first letter.

Unit 2
Core Skills Phonics, Kindergarten

Name _____

Unit 2 Assessment, p. 2

1.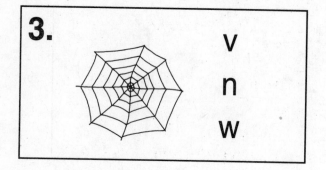
n
m
b

2.
d
t
g

3.
v
n
w

4.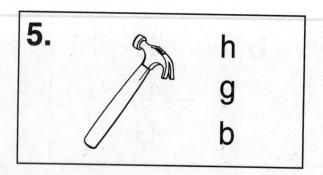
y
j
s

5.
h
g
b

6.
f
j
t

7.
c
g
b

8.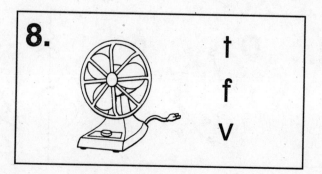
t
f
v

Name the picture in each box. Circle the letter that stands for the beginning sound of the picture.

Unit 2
Core Skills Phonics, Kindergarten

Name_____

Review Short Vowels

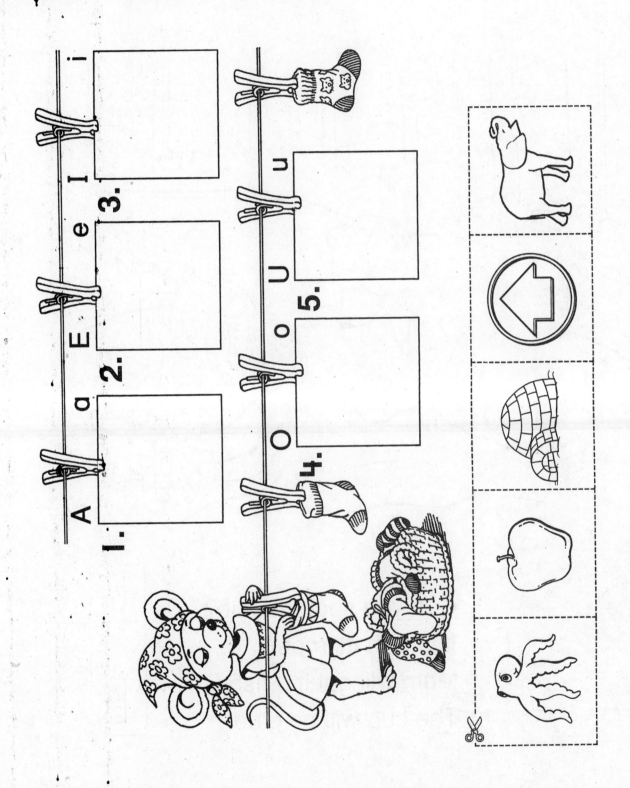

Cut out the pictures. Paste each picture below the letters that stand for the picture's beginning sound.

113

A Cub and Its Mom

Can you spot the cub?
It is with its mom.
Mom will get it a fish.
The cub will be glad.

Read the story. Color the picture.

Name _____

Alphabetical Order

Connect the dots from **A** through **Z** to finish the picture. Color the picture.

115

© Houghton Mifflin Harcourt Publishing Company

Unit 3

Core Skills Phonics, Kindergarten

_____ made this book!

Two Big Shows

Bud's pals get a big hand.

The pals put on a show.

Bud has pals, too.

Quiz Yourself!

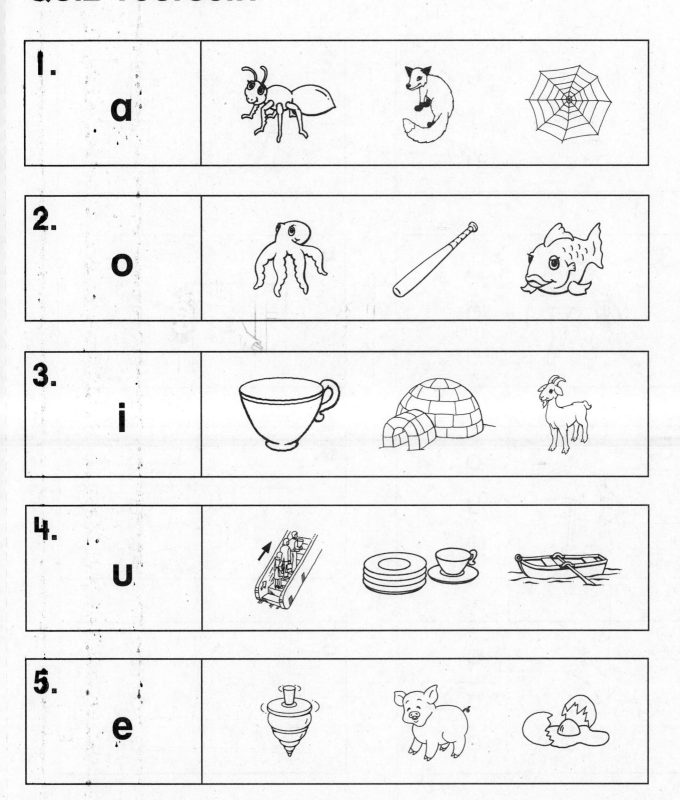

1.	**a**			
2.	**o**			
3.	**i**			
4.	**u**			
5.	**e**			

Name the vowel and pictures in each row. Circle the picture whose name begins with the sound that the vowel stands for.

117

Quiz Yourself!, p. 2

1. 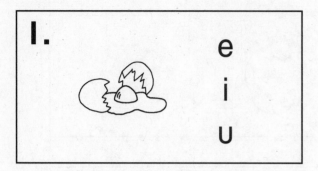   e
                             i
                             u

2.    a
                             o
                             i

3. 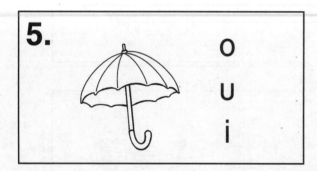   u
                             a
                             o

4. 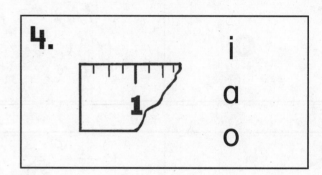   i
                             a
                             o

5.    o
                             u
                             i

6.    o
                             a
                             e

7. 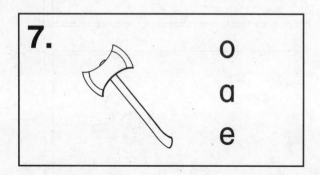   o
                             a
                             e

8.    u
                             o
                             a

Name the picture in each box. Circle the vowel that stands for the beginning sound of each picture.

Unit 3 Assessment

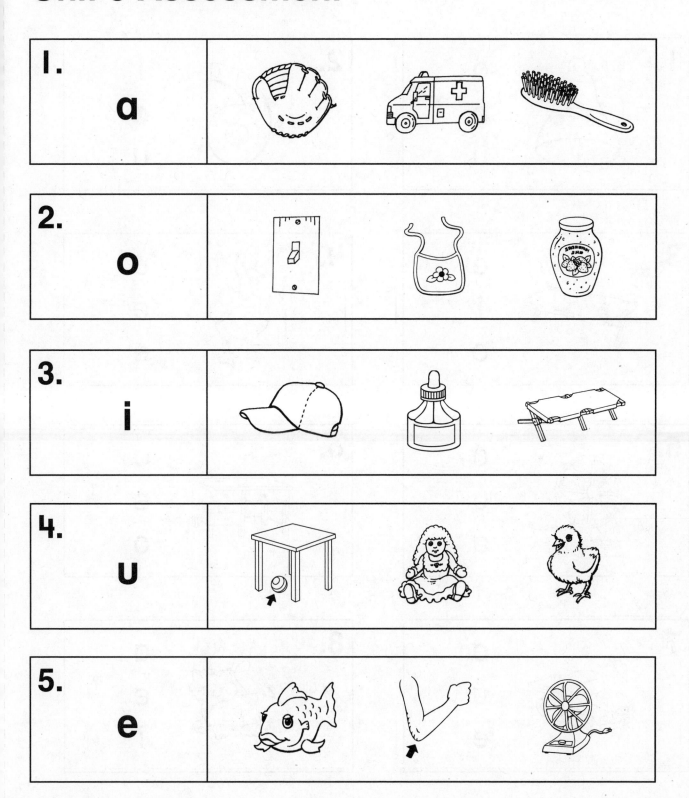

Name the vowel and pictures in each row. Circle the picture whose name begins with the sound that the vowel stands for.

Name _____

Unit 3 Assessment, p. 2

1.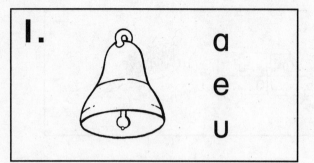
a
e
u

2.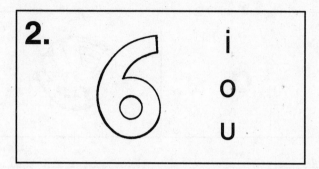
i
o
u

3.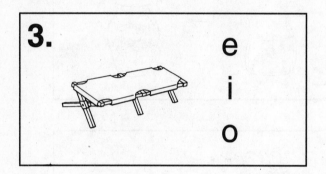
e
i
o

4.
u
o
e

5.
o
u
a

6.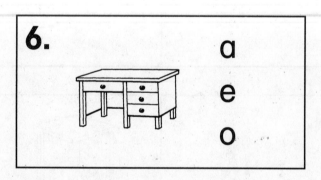
a
e
o

7.
o
u
e

8.
a
e
i

Name the picture in each box. Circle the vowel that stands for the vowel sound in each picture.

Unit 3
Core Skills Phonics, Kindergarten

Answer Key

Page 1
1. *b*
2. *r*
3. *z*
4. *s*
5. *f*
6. *d*
7. *m*
8. *l*
9. *t*

Page 2
1. *i*
2. *a*
3. *o*
4. *u*
5. *a*
6. *e*
7. *e*
8. *u*
9. *o*

Page 3
Children should draw the following lines left to right:
1. from the horse to the barn
2. from the dog to the doghouse
3. from the bird to the nest

Page 4
Children should draw the following lines top to bottom:
1. from the balloon to the woman
2. from the balloon to the boy
3. from the balloon to the girl
4. from the balloon to the dog

Page 5
Children should draw 10 circles total.

Page 6
Children should color the following items:
1. two baseballs
2. two bears
3. two cars

Page 7
Check that children have colored the bowl that is different in each set.

Page 8
Check that children have drawn the following items:
1. two wheels on the van
2. two windows on the house
3. a shirt with a heart on the bear

Page 9
Check that children have colored the item that is reversed in each set.

Page 10
1. chick
2. orange
3. spade

Page 11
Children should color the following pictures:
1. swing, slide, sandbox
2. crayons, scissors, glue
3. ball, bat, mitt

Page 12
Check that children have circled the four children playing outside the shoe.

Page 13
Check that children have colored the children inside the cars.

Page 14
Check that children have colored the parts of the plants growing above the ground.

Page 15
Children should cut and paste the following pictures:
1. fish
2. seahorse
3. octopus

Page 16
Children should color the following pictures:
Sammy the seal, sock, sun, soap

Page 17
Children should color the following pictures:
1. cap, carrot
2. mitt, moon

Page 18
Children should color the following pictures:
1. whale, nail, snail
2. clock, sock, rock

Page 19
Check that children have drawn lines between rhyming pictures and numbers. Also check that they have colored each pair the same color.
1. two, shoe
2. three, tree
3. four, door
4. five, hive

Page 21
1. barn
2. scissors
3. grapes
4. tie

Page 22
1. pie
2. lamp
3. monkey
4. fish

Page 23
1. box
2. boat
3. nail
4. vest

Page 24
Check that children have followed the directions:
An X is on the bird on the left.
The two tulips are colored red.
The wing is drawn on the bee.
The birds and bee are circled.
The rest of the picture is colored.

Page 25

Page 26
Children should color the following pictures:
1. monkey, moon
2. mouse, mat
3. milk, mug

Page 27
1. *m*
2. *m*
3. *m*
4. *m*
6. *m*

Page 28
Check that children have drawn a path using the circles.

Page 29
Children should color the following pictures:
1. duck, door
2. deer, doll
3. desk, dishes

Page 30
1. *d*
3. *d*
4. *d*
5. *d*
6. *d*

Page 31

Page 32
Children should color the following pictures:
1. feather, fork, feet
2. fox, face
3. football, five

Page 33
2. *f*
4. *f*
5. *f*
6. *f*

Page 34

Check that children have drawn a gas pump using the circles.

Page 35

Children should color the following pictures:

1. game, gate
2. guitar, goat
3. girl, gum

Page 36

1. *g*
3. *g*
4. *g*
5. *g*
6. *g*

Page 37

Page 38

Children should color the following pictures:

1. boat
2. banana, bed, belt
3. bell, basket, bone

Page 39

1. *b*
3. *b*
4. *b*
5. *b*
6. *b*

Page 40

Check that children have pasted each head on the matching/correct body.

Page 41

Page 42

Children should color the following pictures:

1. telephone, tape
2. tent, tub
3. tube, tiger, top

Page 43

1. *t*
3. *t*
4. *t*
5. *t*
6. *t*

Page 44

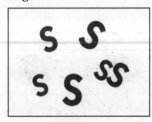

Page 45

Children should color the following pictures:

1. seal, soap
2. safe, sun
3. six, saw

Page 46

1. *s*
2. *s*
4. *s*
5. *s*
6. *s*

Page 47

Check that children have drawn a path using the circles.

Page 48

Children should color the following pictures:

1. watermelon, web, well
2. window
3. wagon, wig, whale

Page 49

1. *w*
3. *w*
4. *w*
5. *w*
6. *w*

Page 50

Page 51

Children should color the following pictures:

1. kangaroo
2. key
3. kick, kittens, king

Page 52

1. *k*
2. *k*
3. *k*
4. *k*
5. *k*

Page 53

Check that children have drawn a path using the circles.

Page 54

Children should color the following pictures:

1. jack-in-the-box, jug
2. jar
3. jet, jump, jacket

Page 55

1. *j*
2. *j*
3. *j*
4. *j*
6. *j*

Page 56

Check that children have pasted the following pictures:

1. watch
2. sock
3. key
4. jeans or jacket
5. jacket or jeans
6. tube

Page 57

Page 58

Children should color the following pictures:

1. pencil, pot, pear
2. purse, pail
3. potato, piano, pan

Page 59

1. *p*
2. *p*
3. *p*
5. *p*
6. *p*

Page 60

Answer Key

Core Skills Phonics, Kindergarten

Page 61
Children should color the following pictures:
1. nail, nose
2. net, nurse
3. needle, nine, news

Page 62
1. *n*
3. *n*
4. *n*
5. *n*
6. *n*

Page 63
Check that children have drawn a path using the circles.

Page 64
Children should color the following pictures:
1. car, cot, comb
2. cup, candle, cap
3. cane, can

Page 65
1. *c*
2. *c*
3. *c*
4. *c*
6. *c*

Page 66
Check that children have colored the correct three hats brown.

Page 67
Children should color the following pictures:
1. horse, ham
2. house, hose
3. hand, hammer, hen

Page 68
1. *h*
3. *h*
4. *h*
5. *h*
6. *h*

Page 69
Check that children have drawn a leaf using the circles.

Page 70
Children should color the following pictures:
1. lion, lips, ladder
2. lamp
3. lake, leg, log

Page 71
1. *l*
2. *l*
3. *l*
4. *l*
6. *l*

Page 72
Check that children have matched hats with clowns.

Page 73
Check that children have drawn a path using the circles.

Page 74
Children should color the following pictures:
1. rope, rug, rabbit
2. robe, rain, ring
3. rose

Page 75
1. *r*
3. *r*
4. *r*
5. *r*

Page 76

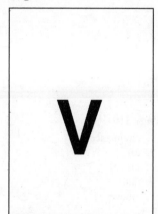

Page 77
Children should color the following pictures:
1. van, violin
2. vacuum, valentine
3. vine, vase, vegetables

Page 78
1. *v*
2. *v*
3. *v*
4. *v*
6. *v*

Page 79
Children should color the following pictures:
yo-yo, yolk, yawn, yarn

Page 80
Children should color the following pictures:
1. yo-yo, yard
2. yawn
3. yolk

Page 81
1. *y*
3. *y*
4. *y*
5. *y*
6. *y*

Page 82

Page 83
Children should color the following pictures:
1. zoo
2. zigzag, zebra
3. zero

Page 84
1. *z*
2. *z*
3. *z*
5. *z*
6. *z*

Page 85
Check that children have colored in 12 sections marked *Q/q*.

Page 86
Children should color the following pictures:
1. quack
2. question mark
3. quarter

Page 87
1. *qu*
3. *qu*
4. *qu*
5. *qu*

Page 88

Page 89
Children should color the following pictures:
1. box, ox
2. six
3. fox, wax

Page 90
1. *x*
2. *x*
3. *x*
4. *x*
6. *x*

Page 91
Check that children have pasted the following pictures:
1. vegetables
2. yolk
3. zigzag
4. rose
5. quilt

Page 93
1. *m*
2. *z*
3. *v*
4. *p*
5. *h*
6. *f*
7. *d*
8. *q*

Page 94
1. seal
2. bed
3. lion
4. rabbit

Answer Key
Core Skills Phonics, Kindergarten

Page 95
1. g
2. r
3. M
4. f
5. x
6. B
7. d
8. t

Page 96
1. m
2. d
3. w
4. j
5. h
6. t
7. g
8. f

Page 97
Children should color the following pictures:
1. gas, jam
2. cap, can
3. ham, bat

Page 98
3. a
4. a
6. a

Page 99
1. a
2. a
4. a
6. a
8. a
9. a

Page 100
Children should color the following pictures:
1. box, sock
2. mop, doll, cot
3. top

Page 101
1. o
2. o
3. o
4. o
6. o

Page 102
1. o
2. o
5. o
6. o
7. o
9. o

Page 103
Children should color the following pictures:
1. fish, mitt
2. wig, pig, bib
3. lid

Page 104
1. i
3. i
4. i
6. i

Page 105
1. i
2. i
5. i
6. i
7. i
9. i

Page 106
Children should color the following pictures:
1. brush, duck, plug
2. drum, cup
3. cub, jug

Page 107
1. u
2. u
5. u
6. u

Page 108
1. u
2. u
3. u
4. u
5. u
7. u
8. u

Page 109
Children should color the following pictures:
1. sled, nest
2. web, dress
3. bell, desk

Page 110
1. e
3. e
4. e
5. e
6. e

Page 111
1. e
3. e
5. e
6. e
7. e
8. e

Page 112
1. u
2. o
3. a
4. i

Page 113
Check that children have pasted the following pictures:
1. apple
2. elephant
3. igloo
4. octopus
5. up

Page 115
Check that children have drawn the ringmaster's coat and pants using the letters.

Page 117
1. ant
2. octopus
3. igloo
4. up
5. egg

Page 118
1. e
2. a
3. o
4. i
5. u
6. e
7. a
8. o

Page 119
1. ambulance
2. off
3. ink
4. under
5. elbow

Page 120
1. e
2. i
3. o
4. u
5. a
6. e
7. u
8. a